Housing Conditions In St. Louis

REPORT OF THE HOUSING
COMMITTEE OF THE
CIVIC LEAGUE OF ST. LOUIS

> Our fight for higher civic ideals will be
> a losing game if these spiritual attain-
> ments must struggle up through filthy
> and immoral physical surroundings

February, 1908
The Civic League of St. Louis
St. Louis, Mo.

HOUSING CONDITIONS IN ST. LOUIS

Report *of the* Housing Committee
──────── OF ────────
The-Civic League of St. Louis

TEXT BY
CHARLOTTE RUMBOLD

PUBLISHED BY THE CIVIC LEAGUE OF ST. LOUIS
1908

S oc 1610.50

Gratis

INDEX

		PAGE
I.	Executive Board Statement	3
II.	Statement of the Housing Committee to the Executive Board	4
III.	Report — Housing Conditions in St. Louis	7
	A. Area Investigated	7
	B. Construction and Sanitation	8

    [a] Lot Crowding:
        Typical Lot — Yards — Yard Drainage — Vaults —
        Passageways — Sheds and Stables — Garbage and Ashes —
        Comments on External Conditions 11-27

    [b] House Crowding:
        Typical House — Apartment — Rear Building — Basements
        and Cellars — Attics — Halls and Stairways 30-36

    [c] Room Crowding:
        Air Spaces — Windows — Lodgers......................40-44

    [d] Cleanliness of Houses and Apartments.................... 44

    [e] Plumbing:
        Nearest Running Water — Sinks — Bath Tubs — Toilets —
        Comments on Interior Conditions.....................46-53

  C. Protection from Fire:
    Building Material — Repair — Porches — Fire Escapes...........54-57

  D. Social Conditions:
    Rents — Nationalities — Occupations — Sickness and Death Rates —
    Police Statistics...59-70

  E. Legislation... 74

  F. Tables 78-84

Statement of the Executive Board

To the Members of the League:

Two years ago the Executive Board decided to appoint a committee to investigate and report upon the housing conditions in St. Louis.

The members of the committee, selected because of their special fitness for the work, were: Ernest J. Russell (chairman), Architect and Vice-Chairman of the Public Recreation Commission; Charlotte Rumbold, Secretary of the Public Recreation Commission; J. Hal Lynch, Architect and Secretary of the Tenement House Association; Geo. Oliver Carpenter, Jr., Fire Insurance, actively interested in social work; Albert T. Terry, former President Real Estate Exchange; Roger N. Baldwin, Chief Probation Officer and Instructor in Sociology, Washington University; Dr. H. W. Soper, who for a number of years practiced medicine in this district; and J. Lionberger Davis, Attorney, actively interested in settlement work.

The committee has made a most careful and accurate study of the housing conditions in the limited area chosen, and the results of its investigation are embodied in the excellent report hereto attached.

We desire to express to Miss Rumbold the appreciation not only of the Executive Board but of the entire membership for the clear, accurate and convincing manner in which she has compiled the facts and prepared the text of the report.

The committee deserves the commendation of the entire city for the time and labor which have been given so freely to this much needed investigation.

We are glad to learn that the officials concerned are framing legislation necessary to relieve these housing conditions and to prevent their future development.

EXECUTIVE BOARD.

Mayo Fesler, *Secretary.*   H. N. Davis, *President.*

T. S. McPheeters,   George D. Markham,
N. A. McMillan,   J. H. Gundlach,
J. Lawrence Mauran,   J. L. Hornsby,
Charles A. Stix,   George C. Hitchcock,
Charles Rebstock,   B. J. Taussig,
Francis A. Drew,   Dr. M. B. Clopton,
Edward C. Eliot,   Henry T. Kent.

Statement of the Housing Committee

To the Executive Board:

Your Housing Committee submits the appended report and expresses its appreciation of the many courtesies extended by the League, and thanks Mr. Fesler for his painstaking and valuable assistance.

While the St. Louis public is under the general impression that we have no housing problems, the investigation proves the idea to be an erroneous one. Many of the evils need immediate correction and laws should be passed to prevent their extension.

Of course, we have not a tenement-house problem such as exists in New York, because our buildings are not over three stories high, but we know the over-crowding of rooms is greater in proportion.

The committee went over the situation in St. Louis generally, picking out the sections which might be investigated, and finally settled upon the one lying between Seventh and Fourteenth Streets, Lucas Avenue and O'Fallon Streets. This section was selected because of the many different phases of the situation caused largely by the different nationalities represented, and might for this reason be considered fairly typical of the crowded districts of the city.

It is our understanding that the following results were expected of the committee:

First. A careful examination of the existing conditions.

Second. To suggest preventive measures and to outline a general policy to be pursued.

Third. To recommend the abolition of the existing evils so far as possible within reason.

The committee, upon the recommendation of Prof. Thos. J. Riley, Ph. D., selected Mr. Edwin B. Miller, A. M., of the University of Missouri, to make the personal investigation. He was efficient and enthusiastic, and the committee herewith expresses its appreciation of his efforts. He made a house-to-house canvass of the entire district, and the result of his work forms the basis of this report. Much of his work would have been impossible, however, if we had not had the hearty co-operation of the city officials. In particular Dr. H. Wheeler Bond, Health Commissioner; Dr. Wm. B. Winn, Assistant to the Commissioner; Mr. Jas. C. Travilla, Street Commissioner; Mr. James A. Smith, Building Commissioner, and Mr. Edward P. Quinn, Plumbing Supervisor, rendered us assistance in the work, our appreciation of which is hereby expressed.

These gentlemen have assured us that they will be glad to do everything within their power to ameliorate the conditions, and we feel that the city is to be congratulated upon the efficiency of its officials.

The committee was fortunate enough to have Mr. Chas. B. Ball, Chief Sanitary Inspector of the City of Chicago, come down and go over the ground with them. His criticisms and suggestions were exceedingly helpful to us in formulating the report, and we extend to him our thanks for his co-operation.

The work of this committee should be continued, and we suggest that it be made a standing committee of the League.

Respectfully submitted,

ERNEST J. RUSSELL, *Chairman*. ALBERT T. TERRY.
CHARLOTTE RUMBOLD, J. LIONBERGER DAVIS,
J. HAL LYNCH, ROGER N. BALDWIN,
GEO. OLIVER CARPENTER, JR., DR. H. W. SOPER.

The Etched Portion Shows Area Investigated.

Housing Conditions in St. Louis

(TEXT BY CHARLOTTE RUMBOLD)

AREA INVESTIGATED

THE area chosen for the house-to-house investigation is that lying between Seventh and Fourteenth Streets, Lucas Avenue and O'Fallon Street—Franklin Avenue, largely given over to business houses, being omitted.

Most of the problems of St. Louis' housing are exemplified here. In other of the low-rent parts of the city there are colonies of people of other races or nationalities who have different social problems—different school, church, health, police problems—but the house problem is essentially the same.

One city after another in the United States finds that that part of the housing of its people which it calls its housing "problem" has come about by almost the same process. A residence district is gradually eaten into by a business district. Some small house district is left on the ragged edge, just off the direct line of advance. The owners, hoping to sell the land for factory sites, are unwilling to spend much on the improvement of a low-value house on high-value ground.

In St. Louis, the old residences downtown on Washington Avenue and Olive Street are in process of rapid elimination, after a period of dilapidation, cheap rents and cheap boarding houses, by large wholesale mercantile establishments. Wash, Carr, Biddle and O'Fallon Streets are waiting for the factories. Meanwhile the aged houses are in a state of almost complete decrepitude, and the system of sanitation held over from the time of village gardens and stable lots has scarcely been altered to suit the conditions of even town life, and is outrageously ineffective in a crowded city.

The district chosen is the largest of the single areas in which the housing is conspicuously bad. The officers of the three prominent charitable societies, the St. Louis Provident Association, the St. Vincent de Paul Society and the United Jewish Charities, consider this the poverty district of the city.

The district covers 124.28 acres—forty-eight blocks. The streets and alleys are 38.87 acres in extent, or 39.2% of the acreage of the whole district, and play an important part in its sanitation. The streets east and west are mostly paved with granite or asphalt. Biddle Street, apparently the coming push-cart street, and O'Fallon being the deeply-mired exceptions. The streets north and south are not so well treated, few of them are paved. The alleys are paved with limestone blocks. Most of them are in fair repair, and often in better conditions than the streets. The sidewalks are mostly of brick. The paved streets are cleaned on an average once every ten days. The garbage is collected twice each week. There are street car tracks, either single or double, on every street except Lucas avenue, two of the north and south streets and part of two running east and west. No district of the same area has so many tracks.

CONSTRUCTION AND SANITATION

Sanitation inside the house, so far as it depends on light and ventilation, is decided largely by the relation of one house to the next—a small house surrounded by larger ones is cut off from the sun and air—and by the construction of the house, the placing of the windows and their relative size compared with the floor space.

Lot Crowding

There are few large tenements, in the general acceptance of the term. St. Louis legal definitions of tenements—there are three definitions—make the term very vague, and in this report it will be applied to any house in which two or more families live and do their cooking separately.*

---

*Definitions of Tenements:

Section 61, Revised Code.—"'Tenement-house' shall be taken to mean a building which, or any portion of which, is occupied by more than two families living independently of each other, and doing their cooking upon the premises, or by more than one family above the first-story, so living and cooking."

Section 194, Revised Code.—"The word 'tenement-house' shall be taken to mean and include every house, building or portion thereof which is rented, leased or hired out to be occupied as the home or residence of more than two families living independent of one another."

Section 629, Revised Code.—"The word 'tenement-house,' where it occurs in this article, shall be taken to mean and include every house, building, or portion thereof, which is rented, leased, let or hired out to be occupied, or is occupied as the house, home or residence of more than three families, living independently of one another and doing their cooking upon the premises, or by more than two families upon a floor, so living and cooking, but having a common right in the halls, stairways, yards, water-closets, or privies, or some of them."

General View of District

The average lot is twenty-five feet in width and one hundred and twenty-five feet deep. The house on the street front is usually the original house, and covers the entire width of the lot. The second house was built on the alley line.

In several instances middle houses have been crowded in between the front and rear houses, and in one case there are four on a single lot. The lower rooms of these houses might, for all the sunlight they receive, be at the bottom of a well.

In this district there are eighteen lots covered 100 per cent by one or more buildings. One solid four-story structure, crowded with Italians, covers by itself 100 per cent of the lot on which it stands, and one-third of all the dwellings in this district, under the most liberal regulation, should not be permitted to exist.

Typical Lot

The typical block presents a solid front to the street of two or three-story buildings of brick or wood. Then another such front faces the alley. Often the people in the alley have a separate address for the postman. It is practically another street. Each house, front and rear, covers the entire width of the lot. The entrance to the yard between the two houses is a passageway under part of the building, roofed over by the story above. The middle building, when there is one, is entered from the yard, as are also the sheds and stables.

Yards

The yard is the center of a good deal of life and excitement. When a group of five to fifteen children, obviously of school age, is found enjoying unlawful freedom in the alley, the explanation usually is, "Nobody in our yard ain't going to school fer a week; Johnny Wolkonskis got the scarlet fever." Crowded somehow between the front building, the rear building, sometimes the middle building, the shed, which may hold men or horses or junk, is the row of privy vaults, the piles of manure, ashes and garbage, the frequent dead rat which lies for weeks, the old mattresses and bed springs, the rags and rubbish, blood and feathers of fowls; and in the midst of it the hydrant, with its broken half-clogged

sink, which furnishes the water, sometimes for all the people in half a block.

No one is responsible for the cleanliness of the yard. Such things as are used by four or six families in common have a tendency to adapt themselves to the standard of the least clean. A total of 1,395 dwellings are served by 664 yards—an average of 2.1 dwellings for each yard. Taking into consideration that these 2.1 dwellings average in turn 2.76 apartments, each with

Offensive Yard and Sheds on Biddle Street.

its family and lodgers, the fact is not to be wondered at that 350 yards, 53 per cent of the total, are marked on the cards, "dirty," "very dirty" and "filthy." (See Table I.)*

There are but few janitors, and these are paid by having the least rentable of all the rooms given them rent free. It follows they must do other work for food and fuel. Their reports, when they make any, have no weight with the agent, and, consequently, none with the tenant.

---

*Tables will be found in the appendix.

Yard Drainage

"Surface drainage" of a yard means that all the waste water from the hydrant and from the slop sinks on the second and third floors, rain-water and melted snow finds its way out across the yard to the lowest level of the lot, and gets out through a hole under the door-sill of the vault, or under the fence to the next yard, or through the passageway into the street or alley, or into the basement. Three hundred and one, or 45 per cent, of the 664 yards are drained wholly or in part this way.

The hydrant sink is a sewer connection directly under the flow of the hydrant. The sink is usually surrounded by broken, uneven bricks, for a radius of three or four feet. These bricks soon sink below the level of the sewer opening, leaving a place for a pool of stagnant dirty wash-water and waste. The complete stoppage of the sink by clogging from garbage, rags and rubbish is not at all uncommon, in which case the ground is again drained by the "surface drainage" method. In many yards the hydrant sink is near the vaults, which act as cesspools for the waste, with the sewer connection under the hydrant serving as ventilator for the vaults.

The yard sink is a sewer opening into the yard, but it is without a flush and often in no better condition than the hydrant sink.

At one place on Wash Street two negro families use the yard sink as a toilet because the nearest vault is half a block distant. Much to the credit of these families the sink is kept as clean as circumstances will permit.

Vaults

Of the 2,022 toilet accommodations found in the district investigated, 204 were water-closets of various descriptions, and 1,818, or 89.9 per cent, were privies, and these serve 91.9 per cent of the population, or 12,251 persons. (See Table II.)

There are two kinds of privies: the vault without sewer connection, being merely a hole in the ground (on Tenth Street an old well was found serving the purpose of a vault), and the vault with sewer connection. This last is often as offensive as the first. The sewer is rarely trapped and is flushed only by

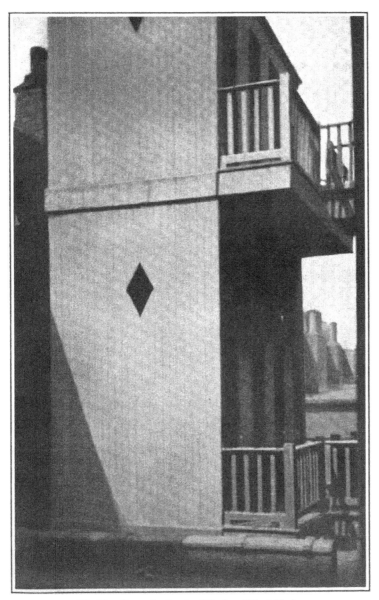

The Two Upper Stories of a "Pier" or "Tier" Vault.

drainage from the roof or the nearby hydrant sink. It consequently adds the gas of the main sewer to its own. In an alarming number of cases the vault sewer acted as main drain for the entire system of roof, yard and interior drainage.

St. Louis, in common with some other Southern cities, has a vault known as the "pier" or "tier" vault. This is usually of brick, built in two or three stories, the upper compartments connecting by bridge with the rear porches of the several floors of the main building, and serving as separate compartments for the families living on those floors. Thus there are three or four compartments, one over the other, and all over the vault in the yard below. If this closet is well constructed and well flushed—which is seldom—it can be kept clean. Where there is no water flush it is altogether unspeakable.

The vault is frequently used as a garbage and rubbish box. In a few cases garbage hoppers, added to the superstructures of the vaults, are the sole means of garbage disposal. These superstructures are often in a most dangerous and filthy condition, floors, walls and seats wet and reeking with foulness. The doors

A Battery of Yard Vaults.

Yard Vaults on Wash Street. The Four Closets Shown Here are Used by Twenty-Eight People.

are frequently gone, sometimes the entire bench seat is broken away or fallen into the vault. Choked with a mass of rubbish the sewer connection is ineffective, and the two kinds of vaults produce in common a foul gas which permeates the block of bake-shops, butcher-shops, fish-markets, and always the living and sleeping rooms.

The 1,818 vault compartments serve 2,892 families, an average of 1.6 families to each compartment. These figures are for the entire district. In the Polish neighborhood the average is 8.7 families. On O'Fallon Street there is a yard where 134 persons are using four compartments (over a single vault), an average of 33.5 persons. This, legitimately.

No one who understands the life of such a district thinks this is all. It is a sad reflection on our municipality that for lack of public convenience stations the men whose work keeps them on the streets must take advantage of the unlocked gates and open passageways to use the vaults in the yard of private houses or saloons. The street-sweeper, the coal-driver, the brick-layer, the peddler, would not be welcome in office buildings or hotels, were there any in this district. Many of the 204 toilets with the more modern appliances are in the saloons—or in houses of prostitution—and are a source of financial profit. The saloon-keepers estimate that one-third of their gross proceeds come from men who feel under obligation to spend some money in return for the toilet privileges. It is more profitable than free lunch. (See Note, Report Chicago Relief and Aid Society by V. C. Hart.)

Many of the worst of the compartment privies are found in saloon yards, where families, for perhaps half a block, must share these closets with "the saloon trade." Where several families share one compartment, the door can not be locked and the "saloon people" use one or the other indiscriminately until all are foul.

Almost without exception urinals are without doors or screens. In all public and in many semi-public privies hang placards advertising patent medicines for and describing diseases of men.

Children live and play in such yards.

These conditions are not peculiar to this district, though they are aggravated by the congestion of population and the lower standards of cleanliness of the newly-arrived immigrants. East of Broadway from Market Street south, from Broadway to Eighteenth, from Marion to Victor, from Nineteenth to Jefferson north of Wash, and in more newly-built districts in the extreme south, northwest and southwest, the privy vault, sewered and unsewered, is still in use and still building. Some years ago an officer of the Board of Health estimated there were 5,000 in the city limits. That was a low estimate then and is lower now, for though some have been closed others are building.

It is hardly necessary to insist and insist that such conditions breed fevers, tuberculosis and hideous unnamable diseases, and that such things spread. In the democracy of the street-car jam we come in perilously close contact with it all.

Is it safe?

More, is it fair?

A Yard Toilet on North Eighth Street.

Passageways

The passageways to the yards are sometimes open above, in which case, though the sun, of course, seldom reaches the ground, they do dry out. If the flooring is of brick they are often clean, and the favorite play-places of the children, since they are cool and dark in summer and out of the wind in winter. The passageway of the rear house most often suffers from use as garbage dump. Sometimes it is blocked with bottles or junk belonging to the shop of some peddler. Sometimes it is subject to abominable abuse of its walls for toilet purposes.

The more menacing passageway is the one leading under the house. This is often the only entrance for families living above the first floor. It is usually very damp. In many cases it is entirely below the level of the street. After a rain such a one is covered an inch or two with water. It goes almost without saying that it is never lighted at night and it is always dark in the day time. It is a brave police officer that ventures into some of these after nine o'clock at night.

Sheds and Stables

Fortunately, it is not often that the stable houses a horse or two, a goat and a few dogs, the peddler's family, and serves as storeroom for his vegetables and fruit. Peddlers, "rags and old iron" men, take the cheapest, and, consequently, most dilapidated sheds and stables for sheltering their horses and stock in trade. These places are badly drained, seldom clean, and the yards around them are damp and evil-smelling. The manure, when it is in a bin at all, overflows an inadequate wooden one. This is usually placed just outside the stable door in the yard.

There are in the district 113 stables sheltering 297 horses. This does not take into account the many livery stables nor those of manufacturing and business firms—only of private stables in the yards of dwelling houses. One hundred and fourteen of these horses in twenty-nine stables—an average of nearly four to a stable—belonged to fruit-venders. Hardly less offensive than the combined stables and fruit stores are the stables, junk, rag and bottle sheds. No ventilation, no light and an appalling smell.

Yard Vaults on Morgan Street. Used by Eighty Persons.

A Row of Dangerous Privies on Twelfth Street.

Side Passageway on North Tenth St. Adjoining Yard Above Drains Into the Passageway.

Garbage Box and Ash Bin

This is a problem not alone of the congested districts, but it is here in an aggravated form. Life would be easier for the people crowded together in these closely packed yards and alleys if they could get rid of the rubbish and refuse. The methods of getting rid of it begin half the yard fights, especially, of course, among the women, and the whole yard combines in fighting the "garbage gentlemen."

It is wonderful how much there is. Broken food and ashes, old furniture—a number of bed springs and mattresses that can be accounted for only on one hypothesis—papers, rags, old shoes, old hats, tin cans, crockery and a thousand other things. Then there are the fruit and vegetables the peddlers can not sell—fruit bought in the next to the last stage, speculating on the chance of selling it before it is gone.

And what to put the garbage in? Buckets, baskets, pans, piano boxes, bureau drawers, wash tubs, hat boxes, trunks, baby carriages, anything of any material, size or shape. Of course, everything leaks, and what of the contents does not fall out is dragged out and fought over by stray dogs and fierce cats and the immense rats that come out of the sewers.

It is difficult to see how in the long run it is a saving of labor to try to get rid of the garbage by putting it in the empty fireplace or the bath tub (this is rare, for the bath tub is rare). "The lady in the third floor back," who throws her "small slop" over the porch rail into the yard below seems much more understandable.

Most often the refuse from the second and third floors is thrown into the porch slop sinks (intended to carry water only), from where it is, or is not, washed down into the vault. Fortunately, in only five cases were garbage dumps found in the cellars. In one case it was found in a cellar toilet having no flush. (See Table III.)

More frequently than is the case with garbage, ashes are found in the cellars. One serious charge against the ash bins and receptacles is their combustibility. Of a total of 524 receptacles and dumps, 331, or 63 per cent, are wooden bins, and 72, or 14 per cent, are dumps against wooden fences or sheds, making a total of 403 or 76 per cent of easily inflammable material and against the law. (See Table IV.)

These notes from Mr. Miller's cards need no explanation:

O'Fallon Street—"Filthy hydrant sink in brick shed."

Biddle Street—"Much rubbish and filth on roofs of sheds."

Carr Street—"Large hole in yard where vaults are caving in."

Carr Street—"Butcher pours blood in dirt yard, allowing it to soak in. Hydrant banked with feathers."

Carr Street—"Urinal drains through yard to hydrant sink."

Ashes Dumped on Roof in Rear of Saloon on Twelfth Street.

Wash Street—"Yard almost covered with two feet of ashes, garbage and rubbish. Stable under rear house very bad-smelling and dirty. Fruit kept here. Dirty dog kennel. Very bad odor."

Wash Street—"Rotten fruits and garbage in stable lot. One seat in vault gone, leaving large opening in floor."

Fourteenth Street—"Air shaft between flats. Tenants complain of bad air."

Fourteenth Street—"Bad tier vaults without flush. Straw dumped about wooden ash bin."

Thirteenth Street—"Rear of house falling. Used for living purposes. Very dangerous."

The Yard of an Alley House in the Rear of North Eighth Street.

A Typical Ash Bin in Rear of Building on Franklin Avenue.

House Crowding

According to the United States Census Report for 1900 the average population of this district per acre was about 180 persons. In twenty-three blocks the density was from 200 to 300, and in five blocks, over 300. The seven blocks from Lucas to Franklin Avenue, Twelfth to Seventeenth Streets, average 246 persons per acre. This was the densest population of any seven contiguous blocks in the city. And this is not the whole story.

If this population were housed in tall eight or ten-story buildings, with ample allowance of floor space, with window space in proportion, and of cubic feet of air space for each person, such a number of people might live healthfully on this same acreage. Of the 1,395 dwelling houses in the district, 1,014, 72 per cent, are two stories or under; 1,390, 99 per cent, are three stories or less in height. Of the 10,744 persons living in the front buildings, that is, those that face the street, 5,322, nearly 50 per cent, live on the second floor, and 9,210, over 85 per cent, live in the basement, first and second floors, for the good reason that there are so few third and fourth floors. In the rear buidings 88 per cent live below the third floor for the same excellent reason. (See Tables V. and VI.)

The possible population of the block, one-half acre, on which the Jefferson Hotel stands, is 950 persons, or 1,900 per acre. According to the United States Census Report of 1900, the population of Block No. 558, between Seventh and Eighth, Biddle and O'Fallon Streets (illustrated on page 47), two acres, was 735 persons—a density of 367 persons per acre. The Jefferson Hotel, however, is thirteen stories in height, and has a basement besides, which gives it seven acres of floor space. The ground space of Block No. 558 is about one-half taken up by yards, porches, outhouses, shops, and two large warehouses, leaving one acre of ground covered with living rooms. Of the 118 houses in the block but ten are three stories high, and altogether they average a little more than one and one-half stories. This gives the block one and one-half acres of floor space. The hotel, then, has a density of 135 to an acre of floor space, compared with the block's density of 490. If the number of guests and attaches at the hotel were multiplied by three and two-thirds, making 3,483 persons,

6,966 to the acre of ground space, they would experience the same crowding which the people in Block 558 now endure.

Even this does not express the discomfort of it. Practically twelve floors, six-sevenths of the floor space in the Jefferson Hotel, is used for sleeping purposes only. In Block 558, less than one-third of the rooms are used as bed-rooms only (the apartments average 2.46 rooms each). In the other rooms the people not only sleep, but cook, eat and do their laundry work as well.

Typical House

The typical house of this district is the old one-family house, which has been converted into a dwelling for several families, and now houses from two to three times the people it was built to shelter. On Wash Street and Carr Street, especially just west of Fourteenth Street, are some of the old gray stone three-story houses, about twenty-five feet in width with the long halls on one side. This style is easily convertible into a house of three apartments, one on each floor. These houses, however, are exceptional. Usually the houses are two-story, with the street entrance up three or four steps leading directly into the front room. To reach the second floor one goes through the passageway into the yard and up the wooden stairs to the porch and rooms above. Where the rooms were originally large they have been partitioned off, sometimes more than once, making the resulting rooms very dark.

In many of the small shops facing the street, the rear portion has been divided off for a living room. This room usually has no window whatever, and coming in from the light of the street one gropes one's way to avoid falling over the furniture.

Apartment

On each floor of the front house there are generally three or four rooms in a straight line at right angles with the street. When this is a single apartment the front room is the parlor, the rear room the kitchen (dining room also), and the one or two middle rooms are bed-rooms. The front room has a window and door, if it is on the first floor, or two windows if above stairs, and is consequently light. The rear room has the same arrangement of door and window opening into the yard or porch. The middle rooms, when the house is in a closely built row—and most of them are—are lighted only from the front and rear. In many of these inner rooms there was not light enough to see to fill out the cards used in the investigation, and a flashlight was necessary in determining the proportion of the rooms—this on bright days. The four-room apartment, however, is by no means the average. (See Table VII.)

Rear Building

The alley house has all of the unsanitary features of the house that faces the street plus some of its own. Its construction is of the poorest. Often the original house has been moved to the rear of the lot, and a new house with a store built in the front. When the house was originally built on the alley, the construction was flimsy because the rent must be low.

The usual height of the house is one or two stories, and it is two rooms deep. The room facing the yard is the kitchen, that facing the alley is the bed-room. Just under the window of this room is the collection of garbage buckets, boxes, pans and baskets of all the tenants of the front and rear buildings. Immediately across the alley is another collection. In summer the stench in these bed-rooms is unbearable.

The cellar of the house is almost invariably damp. The grading of the lot often accounts for this. Surface or defective drainage directs the water toward the rear of the lot, and defective walls and sunken entrances admit it to the cellars of the alley houses. It is a very usual thing to find in the rear of one lot a building or shed whose roof drains directly against the rear building on the lot adjoining.

In an examination of 280 rear buildings, housing 2,479 persons, one bath tub was found—that in the house of a landlord —and four toilets. Only a small per cent of the rear houses have sinks at all, and most of these are defective.

Dilapidation, misery and dirt reach their depths in the rear buildings. The people who live in them are poorer, more sickly, less cleanly and generally of lower standards in every way than those who live in the front.

A Rear Tenement on Eighth Street. No fire escape.

Passageway to Rear Tenement as Shown on Opposite Page

In more than one case the wooden sheds in the yard, meant to shelter horses, now shelter human beings. Sometimes the horses have not been crowded out, the family lives in the loft. More often, however, it is not a family, but a group of men laborers, who either keep house or lodge there.

Fortunately, but two families live in the basements of the alley houses.

Basements and Cellars

In this district there are 107 basement-living rooms—"homes."

It is only in the last few years that basement-living has threatened St. Louis, and it has not gone so far as yet but that it can be stopped without entailing serious hardship on anyone—tenant or landlord.

Some people have chosen to live in cellars because of excessive thrift. They could be moved with real gain to the community. One of the darkest of these "apartments," lighted by two windows, each 1x2, was occupied by the aged Jewish couple who owned the entire building, and from motives of economy lived themselves in the unrentable basement.

There are few children in the basements. Usually the sole occupant is a rheumatic old woman or man, half-starved, half-naked. These people are dependent on charity, wholly or in part, now, and it would be an economic gain to society if it were to take care of them altogether.

The St. Louis' building code makes no distinction between cellar and basement—neither do the tenants.

The entrance sometimes is at the bottom of the steps—basement fashion; sometimes is a double wooden door which folds together across the steps at the top—cellar fashion.

Of the 107 basement-living rooms examined, two are wholly underground, one is one foot in the clear (that is, its ceiling is one foot above the grade), fourteen are two feet in the clear, twenty-four are three feet in the clear, eleven are four feet in the clear, and fifty-five are over four feet in the clear.

Forty-six of these living rooms, 43 per cent, are less than eight feet in height. Considering that fifty-two are four feet or less in the clear, it is safe to say that fully 40 per cent of these basement dwellings could be declared nuisances under the general terms of the law.

Several living rooms were found in which three-fourths of the floor area was used for storage purposes—bananas and other fruit, or rags and junk. Mostly when an old woman lives in a basement she takes in washing. Yours?

Two bath tubs out of the whole number of sixty-five in the district were found in basements—and it would have been better had they not been there. The toilets were worse. Stools without a flush, used as garbage hoppers also, in dark, unventilated corners in or near the kitchens. Such conditions should not be possible.

Usually the water must be carried in from the yard. There are few hydrants in basement dwellings. Of these few, four were found without any sewer connections, the water falling directly on the floor; three of these floors were of wood, the fourth of earth. These must soak up the waste water. In one basement kitchen a broken faucet was responsible for almost two inches of water on the boarded floor. The landlord found it cheaper to lose the rent of the room than to make the repair. Very few

A Basement on Carr Street.

basements used for living purposes had cement walls or floors. Most of the cellar floors which were found cemented were not in living apartments. Usually the floors were of wood—sometimes boards laid on earth floors—but wood, nevertheless. (See Table VIII.)

"Wet" in the table on basement conditions means water on the floor. Taking damp and wet together, nearly 60 per cent of the cellars were in what no one could consider a sanitary condition—not only for people living in them, but for those living above them. (See Table IX.)

New York, Chicago, Philadelphia, Boston, Baltimore and Buffalo require that all cellar floors shall be of concrete of a thickness of from two to four inches. Out of 1,083 cellars, fifty-eight, 5 3-10 per cent, were of concrete, the majority of these in the best blocks of the district.

Of course, such cellars are infested with vermin. Tenants in the negro and Italian districts complain of "millions of big black bugs." These bugs at night are a horror, running about the sleeping room, making a sharp clicking noise. The people say they can not sleep unless they leave the lights burning. Then the rats—huge, gray things out of the sewers. They eat the cats.

Attics

The attic, when there is one, is one of those possessions in common for which no one is responsible. It is a convenient place for the disposal of trash and, consequently, is full of inflammable material. Children play in attics, and the children of this region, as of all others, enjoy playing with matches. The unwatched attic is easy of access—often from the roofs of adjoining sheds or buildings—to the tramp, who spends the night and takes a final smoke before turning in.

Halls—Stairways

There are few halls in the old buildings in this neighborhood. It is in the new ones that the question of halls is becoming serious. The unventilated, unlighted hall is one of the evils just beginning to show itself.

A House on Morgan Street. No Law by Which it Can Be Torn Down. The Shed is Occupied.

Room Crowding

The three and four-room apartments sound "not so bad." These often include, however, rooms not strictly living rooms, certainly not sleeping rooms, the tailor or bake-shop, storeroom, kitchen and the parlor. The parlor is generally sacred from use as a sleeping room. It is a sign of a rising standard of living, but is often—too often—maintained at a serious sacrifice. Also, in general, the more rooms in the apartments the smaller the rooms. As has been said, the old houses had large rooms, and these have been divided and subdivided. A three-room apartment occupying the same amount of floor space as the two-room apartment directly below it, gives the family no more room to live in, even a little less. It does, however, give a little more opportunity for privacy, for the decencies of living, and so is worth the sacrifice of a few feet of floor space. This is especially the case if there are lodgers—and there generally are.

The one-room apartments are the most dilapidated, the worst lighted, the least ventilated, the dampest, and house, as a rule, the most wretched of the wretched—especially if they are in a rear building. A wooden shed on O'Fallon Street, six feet by five feet, and seven feet high, sheltered three people, who cooked, ate and slept in it. One of them died, apparently smothered to death. This is one of the "one-room apartments."

In a one-room apartment there is a bed, a cook stove, a table, some kind of dresser or bureau, and one or two chairs. If the room is twelve by twelve feet, which is large, that is about all for which there is space. The father, mother and children all sleep in the one bed, the baby between the father and mother, the other children across the foot, where they fight for the best position. If there is a girl or boy twelve or thirteen years old, or a lodger, or a grandmother or grandfather, he or she sleeps on the floor. The door and window are tightly closed.

In the morning the family rises, puts on its shoes and is ready for the day's work. Some one, usually one of the children, goes immediately to the grocery store to buy something. There is no room to keep food, if there were money ahead to buy it in quantity. Coal, too, must be bought by the basket every second or third day. Some one else starts the day's water-bringing. Few of the one-room apartments have running water in them; it must come from the yard. If it is winter, then four times out of five the hydrant is frozen and the water must come from the next yard, or a yard half a block away. The children's clothes have all been sewed on for the winter, however, and a washing of the visible parts is all the school authorities require. Breakfast is usually coffee and bread for every one—baby included—and each person eats as he or she is ready and can get hold of the coffee pot and the loaf. The table is never set and the family never sits down altogether for a meal.

Bad as it is in winter it is worse in summer—intolerable unless one is asleep. The parents are glad to have the children out of the house at nights; even the little ones are on the streets. A curfew law to send them home would be a mockery.

It is hard to make more fortunate people comprehend the inevitableness of the friction that comes from living so close together. Everything is visible to every one else, men, women and children. Bathing, washing, changing clothes—no wonder they sleep with their clothes on—birth, sickness, death. There are times when the children must be sent into the street, when the man must go away from the room. There are 435 of these one-room apartments—11 3.10 per cent of the whole number.

The average number of apartments in each dwelling is 2.76. The average number of rooms in each apartment is 2.46 (Table VII). That is, all of the 3,855 apartments in the district average less than two and one-half rooms each. Rooms, of course, are of various sizes. New York and Chicago exact seventy square feet of floor space as a minimum. St. Louis makes no requirements. (Table X.)

This is not the only district in the city which suffers because St Louis has no legal minimum as to the size of a living room. One after another apartment houses in the West End are built, in which the room for the household employe is smaller than New York permits in any tenement on the East Side. One housekeeper declined such an apartment, renting for fifty dollars a month, where the six by eight room opened on a narrow air-shaft, on the ground that she was not going to have a slum in her own house. The district in which such houses are situated has only to become unfashionable to have the apartments rent for less, be occupied by people of lower standards of living, and St. Louis would enter on a phase of tenement-house crowding much like New York's.

The average number of persons to each room in this district is 1.40 (Table XII). A comparison by table of the conditions in St. Louis and those of Chicago (quoting from the report of "Tenement Conditions in Chicago," made by the City Home Association, pages 60, 64, 65 and 66) may explain what these figures mean to St. Louis.

	Average Number of Rooms to Apartment.			Average Number of Persons per Room.			Average No. Persons per Apartm't.		
	Front.	Rear.	Both.	Frcnt.	Rear.	Both.	Front.	Rear.	Both.
Chicago	3.75	3.23	3.65	1.23	1.36	1.28	4.8	4.5	4.8
St. Louis	2.50	2.15	2.46	1.35	1.63	1.40	3.43	3.52	3.43

In Chicago the average number of persons per apartment is less in the rear than in the front building; nevertheless, it is said the crowding is greater because the floor space per room is less. In St. Louis, also, the floor space in the rear building is less than in the front, but added to that there are more people to each room. This is another count against the rear building.

The average number of persons to a sleeping room is 2.69 persons in the front building, 2.97 in the rear and an average for the total of 2.74. The Chicago report calls an average of 2.50 persons to a room "fearfully crowded."

Air Spaces

Room to breathe! The number of cubic feet of air space allowed each individual is the only real measure of crowding. Huxley's estimate of 809 cubic feet as necessary for every human being has been accepted as desirable. New York City tried to enforce a 600 cubic feet minimum, but under the stress of dire necessity now permits the Board of Health to pass a room with a minimum of 400 cubic feet to each person. No other large city permits the air space allowance to fall below 600. St. Louis has delayed too long in the revision of her housing laws. The

An Unpaved Yard on North Eighth Street.

Garbage and Rubbish, Mixed with Ashes, Dumped Against Wood-shed in Rear of Morgan St.

present ordinance is a tragic farce when the municipal officers come to enforcing its provisions of "adequate" and "sufficient." (Table XII.)

Table No. XII shows some of the worst cases of insufficient floor space and insufficient air supply:

No. 1. In this O'Fallon Street apartment a family of three shared their two rooms with two women and twelve men lodgers.

No. 3. The third room here is a kitchen. It is a porch closet 5x4x8.

No. 7. This family of sixteen used only two of their four rooms for sleeping.

No. 19. Two families live in this 12x12x10 room.

No. 21. In this rear building apartment they sleep in one room and sew and cook and eat in the other. This is a "sweat shop."

Such crowding as this is by no means confined to this one district of the city. As in its general sanitary condition and the conditions of the yard vaults in particular, the room-crowding of this district is typical of large sections of the city.

Windows

Because of the churches, schools and mercantile establishments in this district, certain of the more exclusively resident blocks were chosen in tabulating conditions of window space as compared to floor area. Considering that windows mean air as well as light, it seems almost as though there were something to be said for leaking walls and roofs. Fortunately, there are few closed interior courts in this district, though there is a group of new houses on Fourteenth Street with an air shaft closed at the bottom. (Table XIII.)

This is a serious menace—not this one row of houses—but the fact that "modern improvements" all through, not only this district, but other parts of the city, West End as well—too often take the cheap and easy and space-saving and rent-producing forms that proved profitable to some landlords in New York until they were abolished by an indignant city that found they were costing lives.

Yard of Lodging House on Wash St., in Which Forty-Five Persons Occupy Nine Rooms.

A Yard on Wash Street. Six Families in Ten Rooms in This House.

Lodgers

Where there are two or three rooms there are very often lodgers. Then the family practically lives in a one-room apartment—the kitchen—and the lodgers sleep in the other room or rooms. If there is to be any kind of privacy the door must be closed between the rooms. To take in lodgers is the most popular way to reduce the cost of rent. The more newly-arrived immigrants are particularly given to this. It is difficult to estimate the number of lodgers. The householders are inclined to conceal the facts. Every available foot of floor space is used, until there is barely room to walk between the cots. In some of the lodging houses there is a chance that the explanation of the seeming impossibility of getting such a number of people lying down in such space, may be that some of the beds work two shifts —holding one man in the day-time, another at night. Besides being a serious consideration in the problem of over-crowding, the lodger is another difficulty in the way of keeping the children clean-minded—and clean-bodied.

Cleanliness of Rooms—Houses

The woman in this district who keeps her family, herself and her rooms clean, does it at an unbelievable cost. One questions whether it is not one of the wasteful "extravagances of the poor" to spend so much vitality on such a struggle. Could not such a woman help her family more (her family is all she lives for, she counts herself nothing) by spending the strength and passion of work which cleanliness here entails, in earning money by work outside the house, and using it to move and maintain her family in better surroundings?

Some of the good managers wash clothes three times a week, others every day. This, of course, partly because there are few clothes and they must be in use practically all the time, more because the round of work, with its trying accompaniments of soapy smell, steam and wet things hanging on lines crossing and recrossing the room, must be carried on in the one kitchen-living room, where the family eats and often sleeps, and it is necessary to have the process over when supper and bedtime come. That nearly 70 per cent of the 7,458 rooms listed were clean, testifies either to the heroic endurance of the weaker sex or to their lack of economic perception. (Table XIV.)

It is easy to understand why 71.2 per cent of the rooms in the front buildings are clean and but 59.7 per cent of those in the rear buildings. In state of repair, to say nothing of light and ventilation, the average room in the front building is superior to one in the rear, and the problem of keeping the two clean would be quite different, even were the same person responsible for both.

One of the most serious and long-continued wars the housekeepers here wage is that against vermin. Out of the total of 5,592 rooms examined as to the covering of their walls, 3,338, or 59 per cent, were covered with paper, and of this number 709, or 21.2 per cent were in good condition. "Fair," according to Mr. Miller's standard, means "showing slight leaks and breaks." For just what "bad" can mean, one must look at some of the rooms occupied by negroes. In almost every house the walls of one or more rooms are papered with newspapers and scraps of wall paper of various shapes and designs. Mr. Miller notes that he "worked a block in this district at the same time the landlord was having papering done." The paper hangers who were doing the work put the new paper on over masses of other paper hanging in places a foot or more from the wall, without making the slightest effort to fasten same to the wall.

In spite of the fact that the houses in which they live are in the worst repair, and that the walls of their rooms suffer most in their covering, the living rooms of the negroes are almost invariably orderly, and as nearly as possible clean.

It goes almost without saying that throughout the district the old wall paper is rarely taken off before the new is pasted on. It is one of the pastimes of the children to find a loose place and dig down to see how many colors and patterns they can find before they reach bottom. It is a question, also, whether whitewash is very sanitary when it reaches a depth of an inch and a half with all the things entombed in it. (Table XV.)

Plumbing

The trouble with the plumbing laws of St. Louis is not that they do not sufficiently say "thou shalt not"—they are quite comprehensive that way—but that too few of them say "thou shalt."

46 HOUSING CONDITIONS IN ST. LOUIS.

Whatever may be the verdict as to poor plumbing and no plumbing in a village or on a farm, the case is totally different when it comes to two hundred people to every acre.

Plumbing is concerned, first, with having water in the house at all, and next, with conducting the waste matter to the sewer. In the way this last is accomplished, to put it as simply as possible, is the difference between sanitary and unsanitary plumbing. The danger is from the gas which is the product of the decay of such matter. A waste pipe "trapped and ventilated" preserves the household from immediate danger.

Nearest Running Water

Added to all the other difficulties of the housekeeper with the suicidal mania for cleanliness, is the fact that not half the time is the water within her own domain. If she lives in the rear tenement, fifty-five times out of a hundred she must carry her water from the hydrant in the yard. (Table XVI.)

If the hydrant leaks, and it frequently does, the tenants fear to report it to the Health Department, because once this depart-

A Morgan Street Hydrant.

HOUSING CONDITIONS IN ST. LOUIS. 47

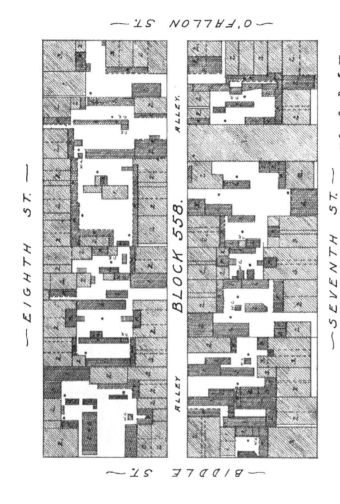

Plan of One Entire Block, Showing Kind of Building, Number of Stories, and Location of Water Supply.

ment notifies the owner or agent of the repair that must be made, the water is more likely to be turned off than the repair made. Time and time again tenants have been obliged to carry water from the next yard because the Health Department declared the hydrant in their yard a nuisance. It seems it is not possible to declare no hydrant a nuisance.

In winter three out of five of the hydrants on the porches, as well as in the yards, are frozen, and the "next yard" of the table becomes three or four yards away. That means carry all the water the household uses for drinking, cooking, laundry and bathing for half a block, and then up a flight of stairs—and then down again, for the slop sink is full of ice. How long would you continue to give five children a daily bath under such circumstances? The woman who does not soon take to throwing her waste water over the porch rail into the yard is either a martyr to self-respect and the rights of others or she is silly.

This lack of convenient and protected water supply is one of the greatest, if not the greatest, hardship life in the cheap-rent districts entails.

Sinks

When the water supply is in the apartment it is as a rule in the kitchen and comes from a faucet over the sink—the usual kitchen sink. The general type is the iron sink with a wooden rim. About one-third of these are boxed in below. This is, of course, not everything to be desired, but generally such a sink, used by a single family, is in good condition. The sink in the hallway, in the cellar, or on the porch that is used by several families, is, as always when things are used in common, by no means as clean as that in the apartment. When the water supply is on the porch, as it is a fourth of the time in the rear houses, it is usually from a faucet above a slop sink. Of these there is one or more on almost every porch.

A slop sink is a painted tin pipe fastened to the porch supports, the top spreading into a tin funnel at a convenient height above the porch rail. There is—or usually was—a coarse sieve where the funnel joins the pipe. It is meant to convey waste water only to the sewer, and so lessen the propensity to throw the water overboard. Needless to say, some one always tries to

see if other things than water won't go through. All such sinks are found on porches and three-fourths of them have faucets opening above them. Not one of these sinks was found either trapped or ventilated.

The contents of the slop sink do eventually reach the sewer, but often by a very circuitous route. The tin waste pipe usually loses part of its load, through leaking or broken joints, before it reaches the ground. In a few cases the pipe empties on the surface of the yard and the waste that is not soaked up runs slowly across the intervening space and empties into the vault.

At a house on Biddle Street two of these slop sinks and three kitchen sinks, the entire drainage for a house sheltering fifty people, empty into a tin house drain, which in turn empties into a hydrant sink, from here into a dark vault built under the porches. Sunlight never touches this damp and dirty vault. The hydrant is the sole water supply for the people on the first floor.

The number of sinks found which discharged their contents into the drain pipes was alarming. Fully 80 per cent of those on the porches of the alley houses did so. Is it surprising that it is hard to keep the alleys clean, or that the basements of the alley houses are so often damp?

Bath Tubs

The short and simple annals of the bath tub:

	No. of Tubs.	Population.	Ratio of Population to Tubs. One Tub to
Front building	65	10,744	165.2 persons
Rear building	1	2,479	2479. persons
Total	66	13,223	200.3 persons

	November.	Per Cent.
Persons having access to bath tub	495	3.74
Persons not having access to the bath tub	12,728	96.26
	13,223	100.

Alley House Between Eighth and Ninth Streets. Note Slop Sinks from Both Buildings Connected with Down Spout.

A Filthy Catch-All-Fire-Trap on North Tenth Street.

It is useless to try to add anything to the force of such figures as these. The investigation had proceeded for fifteen and one-half blocks before a single bath tub was found.

The ratio of one tub to two hundred people is more generous than actual conditions warrant. Twenty-five of the total sixty-six tubs were found in two blocks of especially well-constructed and well-equipped houses. Only one tub was found in the whole number of (280) rear houses, and that was in the house of a landlord.

It may be of interest, though of no direct bearing on the subject, to know that these tubs were distributed as follows: In the

Polish District	1
Italian District	12
Negro District	4
Jewish District	34
Various Nationalities	15
Total	66

Most of those found in the Jewish district were in houses occupied by the owners.

Toilets

In this whole section there are 204 water closets of various descriptions serving 6.9 per cent of the whole number of families living here—the other 2,892, or 93.1 per cent, being served by the yard vaults.

In general, the water closets are found in a few good blocks, or in apartments occupied by the owners, or in saloons. One hundred and seventy-seven, or 86 per cent, were found clean. Most of those listed as in apartments are in bath rooms or partitioned-off rooms, dark and poorly ventilated. In several, especially those in saloons, artificial lights are burning all day. Some are found in kitchens and dining rooms partitioned off by light frames which do not reach the ceiling. (Table XVII.)

There are a number of hopper stools and bowl stools without any water connection whatever. In such a case the condition of the toilet depends on the family using it and the control it has over it. Most of these are on Fourteenth Street, serving one or two families each, and these are as clean as is probably possible. At a house on Wash Street, however, there are a number of this type combined into a pier vault. This is in a sickening condition.

The toilet in the cellar is fortunately rare, but its condition in cases where it is found warrants legislative measures to guard against its increase.

The water closet is another of the "modern conveniences," the introduction of which into the low-rent neighborhoods the city should watch carefully. More than one-fourth of the total number in this district were found in the yards and on porches, and most of these are of the inferior "hopper type." The walls of the bowl of the hopper closet are perpendicular, the flushing usually dependent upon a spring valve or a movement of the seat or bar. Because of rough treatment and inadequate protection from freezing, this mechanism easily gets out of order, and especially in winter this type of closet can be worse than the vault.

Interior Conditions

From Mr. Miller's notes:

O'Fallon Street—"Making sausage in back room with fire falling from stove near kindling and wooden wall."

O'Fallon Street—"Defective sink on second floor leaking through into the kitchen below."

Biddle Street—"Live geese in living room."

Biddle Street—"Walls rotten from dampness. Windows broken."

Carr Street—"Bath tub used as table and slop sink."

Carr Street—"Toilet in kitchen. Entire room smells."

Wash Street—"Water standing on basement floor. Cellar back of basement very damp, dirty and badly ventilated. Bad odor from sink."

Morgan Street—"Walls wet and sagging."

Morgan Street—"Building shaky. Passing car caused one-half inch crack to appear in second-story wall."

North Eleventh Street—"Sanitary conditions horrible. Filth everywhere. Inmates all apparently consumptive."

FIRE PROTECTION

Building Material

In a count from the insurance maps, of forty-two blocks, from Seventh to Thirteenth Streets, including Franklin Avenue, the per cent of frame structures is unexpectedly high. (Table XVIII.) Of course, many of those in the rear are sheds and stables not used for dwelling purposes. But the 106 front frame buildings are probably all so used. It is a matter for regret that the fire insurance companies do not insure lives. Such conditions would never be permitted if these were warehouses sheltering merchandise instead of dwelling houses sheltering men, women and children.

Repair

To the passer-by on the Cass Avenue, the Bellefontaine, the Spring Avenue or the Lee Avenue car, as well as to the visitor familiar with the housing in the crowded districts of New York, the most obvious fact about this region is the wonderful dilapidation of many of the houses—of whole blocks of houses. And a closer inspection makes the wonder grow. One looks at the house, or shed, or lean-to (or at its photograph) with an old shutter nailed over breaks in the wall and pieces of tin covering breaks in the roof, and is sure the next wind will bring it down. "People can't live in that," but people do.

There are many houses through the walls and ceilings of which one may see daylight. In many the plastering is crumbling and falling piece by piece, and each passing of the street cars hastens the ruin. Sometimes the plastering of the ceiling has all but disappeared and the roofs are so bad there is a leakage with every rain. Often the floors are dangerous. The visitor is warned against sagging places which the family has learned to avoid. In such houses the stairways, however, require the most caution of the persons using them. They are repaired with boards nailed on top of the step—on some steps, not on others—are dark in the day-time and unlighted at night. Small wonder the children soon learn to carry matches in their pockets.

The most dilapidated houses of all are those along Twelfth Street, Wash and Morgan Streets and Lucas Avenue, occupied

Defective Flue Through Roof of Middle House, Joining Front and Rear Buildings, on North Tenth Street.

by the negroes. One stairway, which three families use, slopes toward the outer edge at a perceptible angle; the boards are worn and loose and the banister is broken. A child has been injured by a fall and a man has broken his leg on this stairway.

When the cellar stairways are dangerous, the cellar is abandoned—which is one advantage of the cellar stairway over the one in the house. No amount of disrepair causes the abandonment of the house, even though it seems that only the encasing shell of dirt holds the framework together. Some houses, perhaps more frequently east of Broadway, south of Market, have been really abandoned by the owners. The more reason, to the thrifty, or the submerged, why they should be occupied—rent free.

When a house is a menace to the passer-by, when it is in actual danger of falling into the street, the Building Commissioner may tear it down—not otherwise.

Porches

Almost every house, whether front or alley building, has in the rear on each floor railed wooden platforms tacked onto the house, with stairways connecting one with another. These are the porches. The porch belongs to the family in the rear of whose apartment it is situated, though, if there is a third floor, the second floor porch is the hallway for the third floor people, and this means trouble. Usually the porch is the only hallway in the house, and, with the connecting stairways, the only entrance and exit.

The porch is more than hallway. For six or seven months of the year it is the best living room of the apartment. The porches of the front or rear houses face each other across the yard, and the beginning of most of the pleasant hostilities and taking sides that make up a good deal of the recreation of the housewife come from observations on peculiar family or personal habits lightly flung across the intervening space.

The porch is the storeroom, of course, and there are few articles of household furniture that can not be found on one porch or the other around the yard. The gasoline stove comes out in May and the cooking goes on out of doors. That everything around is inflammable, is of no consequence. When it grows quite warm the family sleeps on the porch. The children keep their pets there—pigeons, kittens, and sometimes there are flower-boxes along the top rail.

The real objection to the porches is not only that they are wooden living rooms, but that they are wooden stairways, and the only fire escapes.

Fire Escapes

Not quite the only fire escapes. There are two fire escapes in this district of forty blocks of residences.

There are 382 houses of more than three or more stories in height.

The law requires that every tenement and lodging house which has a height of three or more stories is to be provided "with a stair fire escape attached to the exterior of the building and a staircase located in the interior of the building." (Table XIX.)

The customary rear porch and stairways make an exterior exit; it is doubtful if anyone but the owner of the building would call it a fire escape. It is something attached to the exterior of the building, however. Mostly the interior stairway is lacking, and in only two cases out of a total of 382 three-story houses are there both exterior and interior exits; that is to say, 99.5 per cent are without the law.

In the rear of a three-story tenement on O'Fallon Street, housing eighty people, there was a sausage factory on the ground floor under the porch—the only exit. The large vat boiled away over a hot stove which, at the time of the investigation, dropped live coals near a heap of shavings. This kindling wood was piled against the wooden wall, which reached to the porch above. The only attendant was the butcher, who was selling meat in his shop two rooms distant.

Some of the bakeries are just as flagrant violators of the law, and the rag shops are but little better.

Another law requires that tenement and lodging houses, where the lower story is occupied by a store or stores, or for business purposes, shall have stairways leading to the basement and the second story enclosed with approved fireproof partitions and stair soffits covered with approved fireproof materials.

Not a single case could be found in which this law was obeyed—100 per cent this time, without the pale.

The building shown on page 58 houses twenty-two persons living above the first floor, eight adults and fourteen children under fourteen years of age. According to law, it should have a fire escape, which it has not; it should have an interior stair, which it has not; and as there are stores on the first floor, the stairway leading to the second floor should be fireproof, which is not. This is not the exception among houses of this type, but the rule.

SOCIAL CONDITIONS

Rents

Low rents are the first attraction to such a neighborhood as this; 65.2 per cent, nearly two-thirds of the apartments, rent under $10 per month. The average monthly rental of a room is $4.36, about $1 per week. (Table XX.)

It is instructive to find, remembering what was said of the repair of their houses, that the negroes pay higher rents than the whites, averaging $4.49 per room.

With a few people the reason for living in the region of dilapidation and low rents is the extreme saving, which looks as though it were the fight induced by generations of hourly uncertainty as to the next meal. With most of them it is poverty. The people of small means, who live on small margins, are by no means a homogeneous element, and the problems of their housing can not be solved by any single panacea. One difference between $45 a month and $60—$1.50 a day and $2—is that one man's housing difficulties must be attacked by ordinances controlling the water supply, the plumbing, sewering, light and air spaces in the shop and factory; the other man's trouble, the extension of the street-car system, will somewhat mitigate.

As for the people who live below the margin of independence, the ill, the casual worker, or deeper still, the drunken, the criminal, it is not safe for a city to permit that any of its housing should sink to their rent-paying ability. Indeed, it is not possible, unless, as an indignant Englishman writes, we "build a superior pig-sty." The fact that some people can pay but $2 per month for room-rent should not affect the demand that a landlord put his house into a condition that does not menace the city with

The Third-Story Porch of a Rear Tenement on Franklin Avenue.

small-pox and typhoid fever, even though it raise the rent 100 per cent. These people are carried now by the community, either all or part of the time; sometimes by the municipality directly, through its hospitals or jails; sometimes by the charitable associations, always by individual tenants who pay each month a per cent of their rent to cover losses from the non-payment of rent by delinquent tenants.

A fairly large per cent of the houses in this district are built on leased ground. The owners of the ground are sometimes mercantile associations, which are holding the ground with the intention of building factories and such things when the railway yards and tracks steadily encroaching on the east make them profitable; estates holding for the same reason, or else in probate or litigation; the Mullanphy Emigrant Relief Fund, which, by the terms of its foundation, as interpreted by the City Counselor, may not sell; the Board of Education, a large holder; and some individual owners. The return on the ground valuation is usually five or six per cent.

With a short-term lease, from one to five years, the lessee makes such repairs as he deems necessary in the interior of the house. With a long-term lease, five to ten years, the lessee pays for all improvements, street and alley-making as well as house repairs. When the lease is from ten to ninety-nine years, he pays taxes as well.

If the owner of a ramshackle frame house held on a long-term lease, which had but two years to run, were to be suddenly ordered by the city to pay for a granite street and the paving of an alley, and then to put water in his house, and close the vault and underdrain the yard, and mend the roof, it would be his best business proposition to present the house to the owner of the ground—if he could.

This, however, would be an extreme case. As a rule the leases are profitable investments and, given a short time to make the improvements, the increased return in rent would make them still more profitable.

The usual procedure of the small owner, especially if he has lately arrived in this country, is to buy the property, give a large mortgage and tie up as little cash as possible (the larger

Dangerous Sheds in Rear of Houses of Prostitution on Twelfth Street.

An Entire Half Block of Dilapidated Frame Buildings on Biddle Street.

the mortgage the larger the return on his equity), and selling as quickly as possible at a small advance. Some houses change hands three times in a year. In such a transaction no owner, of course, is willing to make repairs, except, perhaps, to add another layer of paper to some of the room walls.

When he has a little more money, he sometimes buys an old house and makes it over into apartments with "modern improvements," which rent, and, consequently, sell with more profit. If these improvements involve any changes in the exterior of the building, then a contractor draws the plans, and the owner himself buys the material and superintends the building. If the alterations involve only the interior walls, then the owner is his own architect, and he and the carpenter and the plumber make the plans as they work. Or the owner may be architect and carpenter and plumber. Of course, the materials are of the very cheapest, the building of the flimsiest and the planning utterly unconscious of the most elementary sanitation.

Some property in this district pays a return of 15 per cent net. The tenants ask nothing, expect nothing in the way of repairs, and pay proportionately more rent for poorer accommodation than in any part of the city.

On the whole, a reasonable demand for sanitation and repair will not bear too hard on the property holder.

Nationalities

Low rents are the first attraction to such a neighborhood as this; then a colony is formed and another attraction is added, the social. There are people who move from the South Side to the West End because "nobody lives on the South Side;" and other people who decline to move from Carr Street because "everybody lives on Carr Street."

But the same changes go on in Carr Street, the alleys and the boulevards. The first generation of each group clings to it in a custom—or language—walled community; but the children move away and are lost in the last of the huge "mixing pots of the races," the American city. The houses in this district were

A Back Porch in Crowded Section on North Eighth Street.

lived in, about the time of the war, by their German owners. Some few of them or their families still occupy them. One still finds old ladies who say they have "lived in this house for forty years." One house the present family has lived in and owned for over eighty years. After the Germans came the Irish, mostly as tenants. Then came the Jews, once more, frequently the owners. After the Jews, the Italians and the Poles. The negroes, of course, have held on through all the changes.

The Jews live mostly on Morgan, Franklin, Carr and Biddle, from Eleventh Street west. The Italians are moving west behind the Jews. They live from Seventh to Ninth, from Lucas to O'Fallon. Between Ninth and Eleventh is still debatable territory, and is occupied by various nationalities. The Poles stretch along O'Fallon Street on the north (Cass Avenue and north, out of the district under immediate consideration, is becoming largely Polish).

The negroes live on Lucas and Morgan, from Twelfth Street west, and on Wash from Twelfth Street east. (Tables XXI and XXII.)

There are a few Hungarians, a few Roumanians, a few Greeks. These last races, however, have formed colonies elsewhere in the city. The Hungarians, with the Bohemians on the South Side; the Roumanians in the thirty hundred blocks north near Broadway. Of the Greeks there are said to be some 3,000 in the city, and only about ten families among them; nearly the whole number being unattached men, who help complicate the lodger problem. There are some German Jews, a few Galician, still fewer English, moré Roumanian, Austrian and Russian—the majority are Russian. They have, as a whole, the better apartments. Most of the bath tubs and water toilets are in this district. The apartments are fairly large, and there are few boarders or lodgers. The rear building, however, in the districts they occupy, is usually of brick, built to the height of the front building and having a narrow court between. This means that many rooms in both houses are dark and unventilated. The courts and yards are among the worst kept in the whole district.

In the Italian district the alley house is found at its worst. Here are the frame buildings once used as stables, now as fruit cellars, stables, and sometimes living quarters. The single men

A Rear House on Eighth Street. Preparing Spaghetti Sauce.

in this district combine for co-operative housekeeping, instead of doing as so many other newly-arrived laborers do, lodging with some family. Often four to nine men live in a room, and cook and sleep in it—sometimes a day and night shift occupying the bunks alternately. It must be said, however, that the room is generally as clean as can be expected under such conditions. It is in the Italian district that the basement living and working is most common. Nearly all the dangerous cellar bake-shops are found here.

About 50 per cent of the houses in the negro district should be declared unfit for habitation, due to extreme dilapidation. In spite of this the rooms are often pathetically clean.

The Poles live in as nearly the usual conception of a tenement as the district affords, half-block, three-story houses, large families and many lodgers. Where the average number of persons to a sleeping room throughout the whole district is 2.74, in the Polish quarter the average is 3.27 persons. There are but one bath tub and two water closets in the whole district.

Occupations

The sweat-shop, strictly speaking, is a living room in which members of the family, together with other workers, carry on at the same time work taken in from outside, for which they receive pay, and the domestic work and life.

Fortunately, there are not many such shops in the city. But work of almost every description is taken in and performed in the family living room by members of the family. Garments of all kinds are finished in such surroundings it seems impossible they should not carry disease. Not every housekeeper who "sends the wash out" examines the place her clothes are hung to dry.

The most immediately deadly thing, however, connected with home industry in St. Louis, is the dirt that is poured, baked and frozen into the food stuffs manufactured in the dwelling houses.

It is difficult to imagine the dirt in which the wholesale and retail milk, butter, and ice-cream businesses are carried on. The milk is kept in damp cellars, the floors muddy from spilled milk and the water dripping from the ice-boxes. These boxes are never aired, seldom drained, and are unbelievably unclean. Milk can be bought, late in the day, sometimes, for three cents a quart. This does not sour either—in the regular way—by next morning. It seems somehow to rot, if that is possible.

In one block the people who lived there complained bitterly to the investigator of a certain "ice-cream parlor" on the corner. They said that on warm evenings they were almost driven out of the neighborhood. On inspection it was found there was a hydrant in the room but no drain, and the floor, being lower than that of the front room or the yard, the water could not drain out. The half inch that was standing must, on the evidence of the several senses, have been there some time.

Many of the butcher and bake-shops are marked "Kosher," which means clean—ceremonially clean, however, not scientifically clean, and there may be twenty centuries' difference between the two.

The bakeries in the cellars and alley houses are beyond description. The walls, floors, ovens, mixing utensils and furniture are covered with a coat of all sorts of bakery refuse. In the rear of a bakery on Biddle Street the single vault used by all the families in the house was found against the oven, the wall of the oven forming the back wall of the superstructure of the vault.

In a rear house on Thirteenth Street four men were found making tamales. The room in which they were working was black with age and accumulated dirt; there were several dogs and cats, and the floor was covered with "bits of tamale meat and other garbage." Perspiring and unclean, two of them chewing tobacco, another with some kind of disease, they were wrapping the tamales in cornhusks, which looked— — —.

As a rule, vegetables or grapes or oranges bought from an Italian peddler's cart, or lemons from the engaging dark-eyed boys on Franklin Avenue, should be boiled before they are handled. A five minutes' inspection of the homes of the venders would prove this to any inquiring mind.

Sickness and Death Rate

St. Louis suffers from a lack of definite information as to its living conditions, as does, indeed, nearly every city in the United States, due largely to the fact that the statistics gathered by the different municipal departments are either buried by the method of filing, or are not comparable.

There are seven sanitary, twelve police, eleven fire, and ten building districts, and the population is reckoned by wards, of which there are twenty-eight. These districts are all, it follows, of different boundaries. To gather the information for making a definite statement as to the death rate, statistics of sickness, police and fire concerning a particular block for a term of years, would be the work of weeks.

The district under consideration lies in the third and fourth sanitary district. The general mortality rate for these wards for 1907 were 18.50 (third) and 11.80 (fourth, the business district) per thousand. The city's death rate was 14.91 per thousand. "How far bad housing conditions contribute to the death rate is certainly a subject upon which no absolutely scientific deductions can be made." Russell, in his study of the mortality of the city of Glasgow from 1871 to 1880, found that when the average number of people to each room was 1.31, the general mortality rate was 21.7 per thousand; when the average number to a room was 2.05, to each sleeping room, the mortality rate was 28.6 per thousand.

Beside the loss by death and sickness in the usual sense of the term, there is a loss by the lessened productive power resulting from the exhaustion induced by life under such conditions.

One of the things that astonishes the well-regulated visitor on benevolence bent, indeed, exasperates him, or her, is the frequency with which the wage-earner of the house "doesn't feel well today and isn't going to work." This condition is usually laid to laziness and the family abandoned as not being "worthy poor." It is not laziness. The volunteer settlement workers usually last about two years. Those who live and work a longer time in the crowded districts take long and frequent vacations, and guard, besides, with great care, their physical comfort. To live in a tenement house with tenement sanitation and tenement neighbors means a very real loss of vigor and vitality. Sleep does not give it back. If there is one thing such an experience teaches it is why the people are "intermittent workers." The money cost of this weariness and distaste for work is hard to estimate, but would probably be enough in many families to pay the difference in rent for improved quarters.

Crime

The district lies in police district No. 4, in which occurs 20 per cent of the city's arrests, 9 per cent of the population, and 20 per cent of the crime.

Of street-walking there is very little, for which credit must be given the police. Certain streets of the district are largely given to houses of prostitution, and the "lodging houses" are a great problem.

It would be a serious mistake to minimize the personal responsibility of each man for his own conduct and environment, but it seems unlikely that, from the ends of the earth, 13,000 people of all sorts of heredity and racial and national tradition should gather together in one little section of this city and deliberately choose to be dirty and diseased and lazy and criminal and poor.

A Back Yard on Twelfth Street.

A Damp Bottle Yard in Rear of Tenements on Wash St. House is Full of Tuberculosis.

Recreation

When St. Louis was a "city of homes," it was a poor "show-town," also a poor restaurant town and a poor club town. Now that five-sixths of its people live in lodging houses and apartments, there begins to be life on the down-town streets at night.

More than we realize, our expressions of friendship or acquaintanceship are determined by our means of showing hospitality, and this in turn by our house space. One room more or less makes a great difference in the way we entertain our friends. For a family crowded into two rooms, both of which must be used for sleeping rooms, all of this side of the pleasures of home life must be cut off.

If the daughter of the house wants to see one of her men friends, then since the children are in bed and the father is tired, she must go to a dance hall or to a theater, or, what is very popular, make a trip "down the pike," Franklin Avenue from Twenty-second Street east, and take in as many nickleodeons as the couple can afford.

Among the families of the better class or tradition there is a good deal of anxiety until the daughter has chosen her dance hall. The choice of the hall determines the character of her acquaintances, and, quite probably, the man she will marry.

It is no mere coincidence that there are saloons in the district. The saloon affords cheap recreation. It is warm in winter, cool in summer—there is company of one's kind, light and music—all for five cents.

The saloon, besides, cashes checks which, to a person who has never been in a bank, is a great convenience. It is also the post-office of many laborers who, because work takes them here and there, have no permanent lodging.

With the coming of the Jews, however, the saloon is replaced by the coffee house—which is often a misnomer, since there is served "tea and philosophy in the Russian Jewish café and wine and cards in the Roumanian." In the Greek and Turkish cafés there is coffee, very strong and black, and the habitues drink twenty to thirty of the little cups a day.

For the older women the grocer and the butcher shop is the social exchange. All supplies are bought in very small quantities

—it is possible to buy one egg or three cents' worth of sugar—and the housewife often markets before each meal, and all her neighbors do likewise. The tradesman takes a "friendly interest"—indeed, everyone takes a friendly interest.

There is no such isolation as the "roomer" knows. In times of trouble neighbors give help to a proportion of their incomes that would appeal to the most generous of philanthropists.

In summer it is almost unbearable, while awake, to stay in the house. The parents in the neighborhood of Carr Park were unanimous in approval of the grounds being open until nine o'clock at night. This is the time when the streets and alleys are of supreme importance. If they are well paved and clean, there is no greater help to health and comfort.

Some of the Italian alleys are Naples in little. The household work is carried on, the children play, and the babes are asleep on the stones. In the windows there are often boxes or splint baskets or buckets or tin cans, holding carefully-tended plants. When late afternoon comes the tables are carried out and the alley is lined with family parties, resting, drinking, gossiping and playing cards and dice. The peddlers, with their push-carts of hokypoky candy and queer Italian cakes, make their way between. That the garbage boxes are full seems to make little difference.

Churches of almost every denomination are to be found in this district, and, except for Kingshighway, there is hardly any other district so well supplied. There are orthodox Jewish temples. Just outside the district is the orthodox Greek church. The Italians have several churches. St. Joseph's Church has perhaps the largest Catholic parish in the city. Nearly all the churches have charitable and relief societies, and some of them social clubs connected with them. The Jewish Educational Alliance, with the United Hebrew Charities, has a building on Ninth and Carr Streets devoted to the interests of the neighborhood. Clubs and classes of every sort are conducted, and there is a dispensary which does incalculable good. Father Dempsey has a lodging house for men on Sixth Street, and there are several missions.

The Jefferson and the Patrick Henry, the two public schools, are both fine, modern buildings, and both have shower baths.

The city's one municipal bath is on Tenth Street, between Carr and Biddle, and in the less than five months of its existence has proved a success beyond the most daring hopes. Opposite the bath house there will be one of the new small parks, provided for in the late bond issue.

It is to be hoped that some day there will be a generously equipped public recreation building.

LEGISLATION

The conditions of living and housing that have been described are not at all peculiar to this one district. The same evils, though in lesser degree, are to be found in half a dozen other sections of the city, and they are evils beyond the control of the individual immediately injured. They must be relieved by the community for the sake of the individual citizen, and, if for no higher reason, for its own safety.

It is fair to consider the experience of other cities as a warning. New York is, of course, the classical example. The housing there has been through every stage. A description of New York's tenement streets in 1860 sounds as though they were Seventh and Eighth Streets in St. Louis in 1908. "Crazy old buildings, crowded filthy tenements in rear yards, dark, damp basements, leaking garrets, shops, outhouses, and stables converted into dwellings, though scarcely fit to shelter brutes." After this stage came the "double-decker bell tenement," the one hopeless form of tenement house construction—it can not be well lighted, it can not be well ventilated, it is not safe in case of fire—these permit an agglomeration of humanity which exists nowhere else." (New York Tenement House Committee, 1894, page 13.)

Such a condition, or one similar, is the almost inevitable result of lack of civic information and neglect. New York City permitted her low-rent quarters to be crowded closer and closer, until there is no place in all the world so densely populated as some of her streets. Now she spends millions of dollars—after it has cost thousands of lives—to mitigate the effects of her indifference.

Chicago, Boston, Philadelphia, Washington, Cleveland, Cincinnati, Jersey City, have all looked into their housing conditions and taken steps to remedy them.

A Typical Eighth Street Scene.

The problem in St. Louis is no less a vital and serious one. The examination of the typical area covered by the report, in the heart of the foreign section—where from ignorance and carelessness the problem is always the greater—revealed conditions as appalling as the worst rabbit warrens of New York. The great lack of running water, faulty drainage, poor fire protection, unhealthy toilet and bathing arrangements coupled with annual overcrowding in badly arranged and constructed dwellings, have combined to produce a totality of effect to be reckoned with in the vital statistics of the whole city.

The enforced overcrowding of people in sleeping rooms—family and lodger, old and young, among all nationalities—Jews, Poles, Italians, Negroes and Irish—tends hardly more to producing ill-health and disease than immorality and crime. Every fact indicates the abnormality of these conditions. The economic and social misery involved also point to the duty of the municipality to relieve them.

By wise and careful legislation affecting construction and sanitation, by adequate provision for recreation both for children and adults, and by the proper attention to the city's own share—the streets and alleys, the garbage and refuse—such unfortunate conditions can be wiped out and a region of normal healthful homes be substituted. There is no question connected with the administration of public affairs which concerns so vitally the very heart of our community life as that of housing the people.

To remedy these evils so far as possible in the existing buildings and to prevent their recurrence in the new, the following suggestions are made as to changes in and additions to the ordinances covering the subject:

1. That the existing vaults, exterior toilets and sinks be abolished immediately and prohibited for the future, as proposed by the Plumbing Supervisor.

2. That power be given the city to condemn and have repaired or removed the unsafe and unsanitary structures.

3. That water connections be prohibited unless proper sewer connections are installed.

4. That all existing interior plumbing be properly repaired, trapped, ventilated and connected with sewers.

5. That ordinances be enacted defining tenements and governing their construction and maintenace.

The following points should be covered in these ordinances:

(a) Basement and cellars should be made waterproof and have cement floors with drain connected to the sewer, and if used for sleeping purposes should be at least seven feet six inches in height.

(b) Each apartment should have running water, a sink and a water closet.

(c) No room should contain less than seventy square feet of floor space.

(d) Dark and unventilated rooms should be prohibited.

(e) Each sleeping room should give at least 600 cubic feet of air to each occupant.

(f) The glass or window area should equal one-tenth of the floor area.

(g) Light and vent shafts should be defined and made accessible for the purpose of cleanliness.

(*h*) Buildings should not cover more than 65 per cent of the area of interior lots.

(*i*) Porch landings and outside stairs should be considered as buildings where affecting area.

(*j*) Buildings should not be constructed within twenty feet of the center of the alley.

(*k*) Paving and draining of passages and yards should be required.

(*l*) Passageways, halls and stairs should be properly lighted at night.

6. That bakeries, butcher-shops, sweat-shops and the storage of rags and fruit should be prohibited in stables and tenements.

7. That ashes, rubbish and garbage should be collected by the city, as proposed by the Street Commissioner.

TABLES

I. Yards

Paving.	No.	Drainage.	No.	Cleanliness.	No.	%
Stone—Cement	138	Yard Sink	285	Clean	314	47
Brick	519	Hydrant Sink	295	Dirty	211	32
Earth	282	Surface	301	Very dirty and filthy	139	21
Total	939*		881*		664	100

* Where the surfacing or drainage is of two kinds, it has been counted under each head.

II. Toilets

Toilets.	No.	%	No. Fam. Using	%	Av. No. Fam.	No. Per. Using.	%	Av. No. Per.
Vaults—								
Superstructures	1,818	89.9	2,892	93.1	1.6	12,251	91.9	6.7
Water Closets	204	10.1	214	6.9	1.04	1,076	8.1	5.3
Total	2,022	100.0	3,106	100.0		13,327	100.0	

Cleanliness.	No. of Vaults.	%	No. of Water Closets.	%
Clean	1,200	66.0	177	86.8
Dirty	373	20.5	22	10.8
Very dirty and filthy	245	13.5	5	2.4
Total	1,818	100.0	204	100.0

III. Garbage

Receptacles.	No.	Where Placed.	No.	Cleanliness.	No.
Boxes	216	Yard	379	Clean	327
Barrels	135	Alley	233	Dirty	185
Buckets	218	Street	65	Very dirty and filthy.	179
Baskets	25	Porch	14		
Ash Bins	57				
None	40				
Total	691		691		691

IV. Ashes

Receptacles.	No.	%	Where Placed.	No.	%	Cleanliness.	No.	%
Wooden Bins	331	63.2	Yards	471	89.9	Clean	174	33.2
Brick Bins	121	23.1	Alleys	44	8.4	Dirty	117	22.3
None	72	13.7	Cellars	9	1.7	Very dirty and filthy	233	44.5
	524	100.0		524	100.0		524	100.0

V. House Crowding—Front Building

	Families.	%	Persons.	%
Basement	39	1.5	106	1.0
First floor	851	33.6	3,782	35.2
Second floor	1,146	45.2	5,322	49.5
Third floor and above	498	19.7	1,534	14.3
Total	2,534	100.0	10,744	100.0

VI. Heights of Houses

Houses.	Front.	%	Rear.	%	Total	%
One story in height	62	5.6	28	10.0	90	6.5
Two stories in height	705	63.2	218	77.9	923	66.2
Three stories in height	343	30.8	34	12.1	377	27.0
Over three stories in height	5	.4	0	----	5	.3
Total	1,115	100.0	280	100.0	1,395	100.0

VII. Number of Dwellings, Apartments, Rooms

	Dwellings	Apart.	Rooms.	Av. No. Aparts in Dwel.	Av. No. Rooms in Dwel.	Av. No. Rooms in Apart.
Front building	1,115	3,152	7,909	2.82	7.09	2.50
Rear building	280	703	1,517	2.51	5.41	2.15
Total	1,395	3,855	9,426	2.76	6.75	2.46

80 HOUSING CONDITIONS IN ST. LOUIS.

VIII. Basements—Floor Material

	Earth.	%	Wood.	%	Cement.	%	Total.	%
Front building	829	88.1	63	6.7	49	5.2	941	100
Rear building	142	92.8	2	1.3	99	5.9	153	100
Total	971	88.8	65	5.9	58	5.3	1,094*	100

* Eleven cellars were of two materials—generally wood and earth—and have been counted under both materials.

IX. Basements—Moisture

	Dry.	%	Damp.	%	Wet.	%	Total.	%
Front building	384	41.3	502	53.9	45	4.8	931	100
Rear building	51	33.5	91	59.9	10	6.6	152	100
Total	435	40.2	593*	54.7	55	5.1	1,083	100

* Four hundred and sixty of these were of earth.

X. Room Crowding—Some Specific Examples

Street.	Rooms.	Persons.	Floor Area Square Ft.	No. Sq. Ft. Average Per Person.
O'Fallon	2	17	288	16.9
O'Fallon	3	9	201	22.3
O'Fallon	2	8	184	23.0
Biddle	4	16	358	22.3
Carr	1	3	72	24.0
Morgan	1	8	144	18.0
Morgan	1	6	144	24.0

XI. Room Crowding

	No. Persons.	No. Aparts.	Av. No. of Per. in Apart.	No. Rooms.	Av. No. of Per. in Room.	No. of Sleeping Rooms.	Av. No. of Per. in Sleeping Rooms
Front building	10,744	3,152	3.40	7,909	1.35	3,989	2.69
Rear building	2,479	703	3.52	1,517	1.63	833	2.97
Total	13,223	3,855	3.43	9,426	1.40	4,822	2.74

XII. Air Spaces—Some of the Worst Cases

	Street.	Persons. Adults.	Persons. Child.	Total.	No. Rooms.	Total Floor Area Sq. Ft.	Floor Area, per Person Av. Sq. Ft.	Per Person All Rooms. Cu. Ft.	Per Person Sleeping Rooms. Cu. Ft.
1.	O'Fallon	16	1	17	2	288	16.9	135.5	135.5
2.	O'Fallon	1	4	5	1	144	24.8	230.4	230.4
3.	O'Fallon	7	2	9	3	201	22.3	178.6	160.8
4.	O'Fallon	3	6	9	3	300	33.3	293.3	240.0
5.	O'Fallon	2	7	9	2	232	25.7	193.7	106.6
6.	O'Fallon	3	5	8	2	184	23.0	199.0	120.0
7.	Biddle	5	11	16	4	358	22.3	179.0	74.0
8.	Biddle	6	3	9	2	264	29.3	234.6	234.6
9.	Biddle	2	3	5	1	196	39.2	313.6	313.6
10.	Biddle	7	3	10	3	426	42.6	383.4	383.4
11.	Biddle	7	0	7	2	336	48.0	384.0	384.0
12.	Biddle	3	4	7	2	240	34.2	273.3	273.3
13.	Biddle	4	6	10	3	310	31.0	248.0	152.0
14.	Carr	3	0	3	1	72	24.0	168.0	168.0
15.	Carr	7	0	7	1	660	94.2	942.8	942.8
16.	Wash	45	0	45	9	1,780	39.5	350.6	300.2
17.	Morgan	8	0	8	1	144	18.0	180.0	180.0
18.	Morgan	4	2	6	1	144	24.0	240.0	240.0
19.	Thirteenth	5	2	7	2	434	62.0	558.0	558.0
20.	Thirteenth	2	6	8	2	392	49.0	441.0	220.5
21.	Twelfth	3	5	8	2	263	32.8	248.0	105.0
22.	High	5	3	8	2	390	48.7	438.6	219.3
23.	High	6	0	6	2	364	60.6	546.0	546.0

XIII. Windows—Space Compared to Floor Area

	Less than 1/10.		More than 1/10.		Total.	
	No.	%	Number.	%	Number.	%
Block I.—						
Front	43	27	116	73	159	100
Rear	16	39	25	61	41	100
Total	59	30	141	70	200	100
Block II.—						
Front	25	17	122	83	147	100
Rear	5	18	23	82	28	100
Total	30	17	145	83	175	100
Block III.—						
Front	58	19	242	81	300	100
Rear	1	7	13	93	· 14	100
Total	59	19	255	81	314	100
Block IV.—						
Front	32	12	244	88	276	100
Rear	6	9	62	91	68	100
Total	38	11	306	89	344	100
Block V.—						
Front	43	18	203	82	246	100
Rear	5	12	35	88	40	100
Total	48	17	238	83	286	100
Five blocks—Total	234	18	1,085	82	1,319	100

XIV. Cleanliness of Rooms and Apartments

Rooms.	Clean.	%	Dirty.	%	Very Dirty and Filthy	%	Total.	%
Front building	4,536	71.2	1,438	22.5	400	6.3	6,374	100
Rear building	647	59.7	330	30.4	107	9.9	1,084	100
Total	5,183	69.5	1,768	23.7	507	6.8	7,458	100

XV. Covering of Walls

	Good.	%	Fair.	%	Bad and Very Bad.	%	Total.
Paper	709	21.2	1,808	54.2	821	24.6	3,338—100 per ct.
Whitewash	669	20.7	992	44.0	593	26.3	2,254—100 per ct.
Total	1,378	22.8	2,800	51.9	1,414	25.3	5,592—100 per ct.

XVI. Nearest Running Water

	Within Apart.		Hall.		Porch.		Next Floor.		Yard.		Next Yard.		Total.	
	No.	%	No.	%	No.	%	No.	%	No.	%	No	%	No.	%
Front Building	1561	49.4	84	2.7	594	18.8	127	40	734	23.2	61	1.9	3161	100
Rear Building	123	17.4	1	0.2	174	24.7			390	55.3	17	2.4	705	100
Total	1684	43.6	85	2.2	768	19.9	127	3.3	1124	29.0	78	2.0	3866	100

XVII. Location of Water Closets

Location.	Number.	Per Cent.
Apartment	130	63.7
Hall	10	4.9
Cellar	8	3.9
Porch	42	20.6
Yard	14	6.9
Total	204	100.0

XVIII. Building Material

	Brick.	%	Frame.	%	Total.	%
Front	1,424	93	106	7	1,530	100
Rear	406	62	254	38	660	100
Mercantile	78	70	33	30	111	100
Total	1,908	83	393	17	2,301	100

XIX. Fire Escapes

Three-story and over three-story houses required by law to have fire escapes on outside of building.

Number having	2	.5 per cent
Number not having	380	99.5 per cent
Total	382	100.0 per cent

XX. Apartments Renting

Amount Per Month.	Number.	Per Cent.
Under $4.00	201	7.1
$4.00—$5.99	366	12.9
$6.00—$7.99	658	23.3
$8.00—$9.99	617	21.9
$10.00 and over	984	34.8
Total	2,826	100.0

XXI. Nationalities

Nationalities.	Front Building.				Rear Building.				Total.				Average No. of Persons in Family.
	Fams.		Persons.		Fams.		Persons.		Families.		Persons.		
	No.	%	No.	%	No.	%	No.	%	No.	%	No.	%	
Jews	795	31.4	3,065	28.5	215	31.5	681	27.5	1,010	31.4	3,746	28.4	3.7
Italians	592	23.4	3,005	28.0	147	21.5	643	25.9	739	23.0	3,648	27.5	4.9
Negroes	452	17.8	1,763	16.4	105	15.4	315	12.7	557	17.3	2,078	15.7	3.7
Various Nat's	428	16.2	1,670	15.5	104	15.2	354	14.3	532	16.5	2,024	15.3	3.8
Poles	267	10.5	1,241	11.6	112	16.4	486	19.6	379	11.8	1,727	13.1	4.5
Total	2534	100.0	10,744	100.0	683	100.0	2,479	100.0	3,217	100.0	13,223	100.0	4.1

XXII. Children Under Fourteen Years of Age

Nationalities.	Adults.	%	Children Under 14 Years.	%	Total.	Ratio— One Child to Adult.
Jews	2,559	68.6	1,187	31.4	3,746	2.1
Italians	2,694	73.8	954	26.2	3,648	2.8
Negroes	1,752	84.3	326	15.7	2,078	5.3
Various Nat's	1,728	85.4	296	14.6	2,024	5.8
Poles	1,286	75.5	441	25.5	1,727	2.9
Total	10,019	75.8	3,204	24.2	13,223	3.1

Officers of the League

President
H. N. DAVIS

Secretary
MAYO FESLER, Security Building

Treasurer
N. A. MCMILLAN

Vice-Presidents

T. S. MCPHEETERS	CHARLES NAGEL
ROBERT MOORE	F. N. JUDSON
EDW. MALLINCKRODT	GUSTAV CRAMER

Executive Board

T. S. McPheeters	Geo. D. Markham
N. A. McMillan	J. H. Gundlach
J. Lawrence Mauran	Joseph L. Hornsby
Charles A. Stix	B. J. Taussig
Charles Rebstock	Dr. M. B. Clopton
F. A. Drew	George C. Hitchcock
Edward C. Eliot	Henry T. Kent

Counsel

B. Schnurmacher	Luther Ely Smith

Honorary Auditors
Jones, Cæsar, Dickinson, Wilmot & Co.

Advisory Council

George L. Allen	Clarence H. Howard
Thekla M. Bernays	C. H. Huttig
W. K. Bixby	Wm. B. Ittner
T. B. Boyd	Henry Leschen
Robert S. Brookings	Julius Lesser
Paul Brown	Homer P. Knapp
Adolphus Busch	Mrs. L. M. McCall
James M. Byrnes	Hugo Muench
Mrs. Geo. O. Carpenter	Hugh McKittrick
Murray Carleton	Mrs. T. H. McKittrick
Daniel Catlin	Mrs. Philip N. Moore
Charles Clark	Elias Michael
Hanford Crawford	Dan C. Nugent
C. C. Crone	Mrs. Everett W. Pattison
Frank P. Crunden	B. Schnurmacher
Rev. John W. Day	James E. Smith
George F. Durant	Mrs. Edward Taussig
B. F. Edwards	John H. Terry
Geo. L. Edwards	Bishop Dan'l S. Tuttle
Mrs. W. E. Fischel	Louis H. Waltke
Mrs. John Fowler	Edwards Whitaker
David R. Francis	Henry Wood
S. H. Fullerton	Louis Werner
Henry F. Hafner	George M. Wright

Edmund H. Wuerpel

Committees of the League

Press, Publication and Public Meetings
CHAS. A. STIX, Chairman
Hanford Crawford   Chas. W. Nugent
George M. Wright   James E. Smith

Membership and Organization
J. H. GUNDLACH, Chairman
Joseph R. Barroll   Earl Layman
Ernest M. Link   A. H. Foote
A. H. Richardson   Chas. P. Pettus
H. H. Oberschelp   J. Hugo Grimm
Otto G. Koenig   George W. Lubke

Municipal and State Legislation
GEO. C. HITCHCOCK, Chairman
W. Palmer Clarkson   O. L. Teichmann
J. Clarence Taussig   J. F. O. Reller
J. L. Hornsby   Lambert E. Walther

Charter Revision
F. N. JUDSON, Chairman
Clifford B. Allen   Robert Moore
Geo. D. Markham   Edw. C. Eliot
Edw. J. McCullen   Dr. John C. Morfit

Public Sanitation
J. HAL LYNCH, Chairman
Thos. D. Cannon   O. J. Wilhelmi
Dr. Nathaniel Allison   Dr. Joseph Spiegelhalter
S. M. Coulter   Geo. W. Sutherland
John H. Terry

Smoke Abatement
OSCAR L. WHITELAW, Chairman
Wm. H. Bryan   Geo. W. Parker
Calvin M. Woodward   J. B. Conroy
Wm. Chauvenet   Dr. Bransford Lewis

Tree Planting
DR. SELDEN SPENCER, Chairman
Dr. H. A. Geitz   Chas. Rebstock
W. J. Stevens   Frank A. Weber
H. C. Irish

Historic Sites
PIERRE CHOUTEAU, Chairman
W. S. Bedal   Dr. Edw. Evers
Walter B. Douglas   Mrs. W. E. Fischel
Walter R. Smith   Marshall S. Snow
Joseph Boyce

Housing
ERNEST J. RUSSELL, Chairman
J. Hal Lynch   Charlotte M. Rumbold
Albert T. Terry   J. Lionberger Davis
R. N. Baldwin   Geo. Oliver Carpenter, Jr.
Dr. H. W. Soper

Committees of the League—Continued

Eleemosynary Institutions

O'NEILL RYAN, Chairman

W. S. Eames
E. M. Grossman
W. Banks Rogers
Dr. M. B. Clopton

Dr. Robert Luedeking
Dr. Sidney I. Schwab
Dr. John Green, Jr.

Signs and Billboards

L. L. LEONARD, Chairman

Daniel N. Kirby
John H. Roth
Robert Rutledge

Louis Spiering
Frederick M. Mann
M. Schoenberg

City Plan

JOHN F. LEE, Chairman

Enos Clarke
James E. Hereford
George E. Kessler
Dr. Samuel J. Will
John Fowler
Julius Pitzman

Philip C. Scanlan
Chas. Nagel
David R. Francis
Halsey C. Ives
Col. E. J. Spencer

Parks and Public Grounds

HENRY T. KENT, Chairman

Lewis D. Dozier
John E. McKinney
Eugene S. Wilson
Edward F. Goltra

C. H. McMillan
Robert McCulloch
William Trelease
Theophilus Conzelman

City Lighting

J. L. VAN ORNUM, Chairman

E. L. Adreon
A. S. Langsdorf
Joseph D. Bascom

Arthur Thacher
Trescott F. Chaplin
John J. Lichter

Theater Building Regulations

WARREN TYRRELL, Chairman

Gouverneur Calhoun
Otto Heller
Wilbur T. Trueblood

T. S. McPheeters, Jr.
Sterling Edmunds
Louis La Beaume

Street Improvements

W. P. H. TURNER, Chairman

J. Charless Cabanne
James C. Travilla
Edward Flad
Hermann von Schrenk

Guy C. Mariner
Henry Wright
Fred. G. Ziebig

Municipal Discussions

V. MOTT PORTER, Chairman

Paul Blackwelder
Rev. Geo. R. Dodson
Dwight F. Davis

Wm. B. Ittner
Wm. L. Gifford
Dr. B. W. Moore

The Civic League of St. Louis

What the League is

The Civic League of St. Louis is an independent non-partisan association designed to unite the efforts of all citizens who are seeking to improve municipal conditions in this City.

Its General Purposes are

To labor for the enactment and strict enforcement of laws.

To create public sentiment in favor of better municipal conditions and to crystallize that sentiment into action.

To serve as a bureau of civic information to the citizens.

To support every movement which will make St. Louis a more healthful, comfortable and attractive city.

How the League is Supported

The League is everybody's League, and welcomes to its ranks every honest and public-spirited citizen, whatever may be the measure of his financial ability.

It is supported solely by membership dues and the voluntary contributions of those who believe in its work.

Membership

Any citizen of St. Louis or its suburbs can become a member by paying the annual membership dues.

Regular Membership	$ 2 00
Contributing Membership	5 00
Sustaining Membership	10 00
Honorary Membership	25 00
Patron	100 00

CPSIA information can be obtained
at www.ICGtesting.com
Printed in the USA
LVHW031808240223
740366LV00012B/668